Yuba Flows

Poetry by
Kirsten Casey, Gary Cooke, Cheryl Dumesnil,
Judy Halebsky, Iven Lourie & Scott Young

Yuba Flows

Poetry by
Kirsten Casey, Gary Cooke, Cheryl Dumesnil,
Judy Halebsky, Iven Lourie & Scott Young

Edited by Gail Rudd Entrekin

HPP
HIP POCKET PRESS

Managing Editor, Charles Entrekin
Nevada City, CA
2007

Copyright 2007 by Hip Pocket Press

Hip Pocket Press
228 Commercial Street, #138
Nevada City, CA 95959

Typesetting by Wordsworth
          San Geronimo, CA

Printing and distribution by Lightning Source, Inc.

Cover design by Brook Design Group
          Nevada City, CA

Cover photo, "Yuba Flows," by David McKay
          www.davidmckayphotography.com

Order at www.hippocketpress.com

ISBN 0-917658-35-3

Acknowledgements

Gary Cooke

"The Big Blue Ball" (Farfelu, 2005)
"Bits of Glass" (Sierra Journal, 2003)
"Dead Poem" (Farfelu, 2006)
"The Road Between Them" from *Sierra Songs & Descants* (Hip Pocket Press, 2002)
"This Part of Texas" (Borderlands: Texas Poetry Review, Spring 2007)
"The Windows" from *Nevada County Poetry Anthology* (Nevada County Poetry Series, 2002)

Cheryl Dumesnil

"Somewhere in a Box Marked Keep" (poemmemoirstory, 2002)
"Creature" (Barrow Street, 2002)
"Narrative" (Gargoyle, 2003)
"Revisited" (Hootenanny, 1995)
"Say Yes" (Many Mountains Moving, 1999, under the title "Dark Night, Cool Water")
"When" (Nimrod International Journal, 2004)

Judy Halebsky

"Oh sky, a little bit even, fly not"(Five Fingers Review, 2006)
"On the Coast," "The Big School" (Mamazine, 2005)
"Purcell's Cove Road" (New Delta Review, 1998)
"Red Hollow," "Down the Mountain" (Artmatters, 2006)
"Thinned by Storm" (Poetry Now, 2007)
"Whale Music" (Eleven Eleven {1111} 2004)

Iven Lourie

"A Question of Memory," "Daughter of Aeolus" (Natural Bridge, Special Dreams Issue, 2006)
"Comprehension" (Poetry-Chicago, 1968)
"Growing Older Here" from *Nevada County Poetry Anthology* (Nevada County Poetry Series, 2001)
"Lee Bontecou Show at the Museum of Contemporary Art, Chicago" (Sierra Journal, 2007)

Contents

Publishers Preface   13

Cheryl Dumesnil
Meteorology   17
Junk Shop Magic   19
The Swimmer   20
Revisited   21
Recurring   22
Somewhere in a Box Marked Keep   23
Narrative   24
When   26
Other Nights   28
If   29
Creature   30
Q to the 6 Train   31
Getting It Right This Time   33
Dark Magic   34
Say Yes   36

Gary Cooke
After Seeing 'Edward Hopper, The Paris Years'   39
Art Show   40
Backyard in Summer   41
Biting at the Rain   42
The Big Blue Ball   43
Bits of Glass   44
Dead Poem   45
The Curve of Earth   47

Ducks Leaving   48
Flying Fox   49
King of the Rooftop   50
Koi Pond   51
The Question   52
Red Moon   53
The Road Between Them   54
This Part of Texas   55
What I remember   56
The Windows   57
Your Smile   58

Judy Halebsky

Lay it down   61
お空はちょっとも飛べない
Oh sky, a little bit even, fly not   66
楚 Woman Under Trees   67
My Father Remembers Blue Zebras   68
Thinned by Storm   69
Whale Music   70
On the Coast   73
Landscape   74
The Big School   75
Monster Walking in a Snowstorm with Feet Tied Together (a painting)   76
Daddy says he teaches people about people   77
Purcell's Cove Road   78
(notes on why)   79
Red Hollow   80
Down the Mountain   81

Scott Young
The Language of Longing   85
Winter Morning Walk   87
Why I Climb Mountains   88
The Heron   90
My Cat Asks a Question   91
Restless Invitation   92
"The Pumpkin Knew Too Much"   93
The Kiss   94
Late Night Violin Practice with Margarita   95
Imagined Anniversary   97
I Love My Penis   99
Forsythia   100
A Mother's Death   101
Dusk and Silence   103
Cold   104

Kirsten Casey
Bad Girl   107
Maxine remembers the goats   108
1976 Gonzales, California   109
J.M. Barrie   110
Painless   111
A question that you should say yes to   113
Take it back,   114
Bachelor Party   116
Falling Senseless   117
Reunion of the Separated   118
An inebriated monk illuminating a great text   120
In a Goddamn Hotel Room   121
The right way to say goodbye   123
Sound   125
Obituary for a New York Corpse   126

Iven Lourie
The Days of Awe
    I. Rosh Hashannah   129
    II. The Raven   130
    III. Monday, September 12, 1994   131
    IV. Inventing the Pleasures   132
    V. Honor Among Ghosts   133
    VI. Fire Reflected in Water—*Yom Kippur* (Day of Atonement)   135
A Question of Memory   136
The Daughter of Aeolus   138
Comprehension   139
Lee Bontecou Show at the Museum of Contemporary Art, Chicago   140
Winter Solstice   142
The Letting Go   145
Growing Older Here   147

Hip Pocket Press Mission Statement

It is our belief that the arts are the embodiment of the soul of a culture, that the promotion of writers and artists is essential if our current culture, with its emphasis on television and provocative outcomes, is to have a chance to develop that inner voice and ear that expresses and listens to beauty. Toward that end, Hip Pocket Press will search out those undiscovered poets and writers whose voices can give us a clearer understanding of ourselves and of the culture which defines us.

It is difficult
to get the news from poems
yet men die miserably every day
for lack
of what is found there.

William Carlos Williams

Publisher's Preface

These six poets represent, we believe, a style that deserves recognition and celebration; a style peculiar to an aesthetic one finds most often in the Northwestern United States. It is a style that is place-based, character-based, and story-based. It eschews the emptiness of abstractions, the social pressure of political correctness, and the simpering, wayward sentimentalities of postmodern authorial intrusions. This style of writing believes that beneath every human phenomenon lies concealed a discrepant reality, and that an advantage can be gained by bringing it to light, by "going under the surface" and bringing that discrepant piece of the puzzle up into consciousness. This kind of writing bears up under scrutiny; it reveals what is necessary for us all to know; it returns benefit for effort; it is a joy to behold; and it reminds us, finally, what is most gratifying to know—that we are a part of a larger reality, that we are not alone.

Charles Entrekin
Managing Editor
Hip Pocket Press

Cheryl Dumesnil

Q to the 6 Train

You may do this, I tell you, it is permitted.
Begin again the story of your life.

— Jane Hirshfield, "Da Capo"
Lives of the Heart (Harper Perennial, 1997)

Cheryl Dumesnil's poems have appeared in *Bakunin, Barrow Street, Nimrod, Calyx,* and other literary magazines. Her books include *Dorothy Parker's Elbow: Tattoos on Writers, Writers on Tattoos* (Warner 2002) which she edited with Kim Addonizio, and *Hitched! Wedding Stories from San Francisco City Hall* (Thunder's Mouth 2005). She lives in Walnut Creek, California, with her wife Tracie and their two sons.

Meteorology

The year I got divorced, El Niño slammed
the California coast and for a while everything

changed—salmon boats hauled tropical fish
out of San Francisco Bay, a partridge native

to North Dakota pecked around my front stoop,
escapee from a Chinatown butcher shop, or

benefactor of some misguided wind. North
of here, a small town slid into Russian River,

A-frame cabins, redwood decks and all, while
fundamentalists preached Armageddon, and I

learned to cook single portions, to say I
instead of we. Mornings, a waterfall poured

from my neighbor's roof past my bedroom
window, and I woke up feeling like a woman

who had let her disaster insurance lapse
just before the storm, or that person you see

on the news, slogging through her basement
in borrowed hip waders, showing the camera

a soggy cardboard box, crying, *Twenty years
of photographs . . . it's a shame.* Over coffee

a friend told me, *I am so glad I got married
then divorced*, and I wondered if I would ever

feel the same. Most nights I worked late,
listening to traffic reports, waiting for a break

in the weather, while students huddled under
umbrellas shuffled past my office door

to the library, the cafeteria, the party or dorm.
Driving home one night, I watched a Nissan

throw arabesques and pirouettes around
four lanes of traffic, then land on the graveled

shoulder in text-book parallel parking fashion,
totally unscathed. Two miles later a sedan glided

so gracefully off the freeway, I wondered if
I had really seen it at all—two red lights arcing

down the ice plant embankment, the sound
of its impact absorbed by rain. I drove home

ditching potholes and fallen limbs, expecting
anything to happen next—a stranger's face

appearing in my rearview mirror, a woman
descending from the clouds, muttering my name.

Junk Shop Magic

The magician pulled his gingham napkin
off the three-legged table: *Voilá!* He said,

Your soul: a crag of obsidian displayed
on the up-turned butt of a dime-store cup.

Tule fog scratched at the basement's
locked door. Shouldn't it be a baseball-sized

emerald? Precision-cut facets of a ruby
throwing off light? He coughed, *Here's*

what you got, lit a Kool, then snapped
two fingers and disappeared into his hat.

I closed up shop, spent the night
hunkered on a stack of junk yard bricks,

skirt hem polishing my dull black rock.

The Swimmer

Teal river water, backdrop
    of evergreens arrowed upward,
        that early mountain light,

and she is in the center, waist-deep
    in her lavender suit, rubbing water
        between prayer hands, her hair

the color of redwood bark. She has
    given up on love, this morning's
        solo swim is the last broken promise

she'll make the best of. In the next
    frame, a local kid scuffles down
        the riverbank, plants her body

on a boulder and starts picking
    acoustic notes out of old
        guitar strings, her

sneakered foot tapping up
    a rhythm of dust. Filtered light
        netting the river, minnows

eating algae off rocks by her feet—
    the swimmer is pulling
        small graces from water,

from the canopy of song overhead.

Revisited

What is desire but the wish for some
relief from the self.
         Stephen Dobyns, "Desire"
              Body Traffic (Puffin, 1991)

Two days into my cross-country drive,
nothing between my dirt-specked windshield
and the horizon's chiseled bluffs
but baked flat land, Wyoming-blue sky

and this: a dust cloud spinning
above the valley floor—each particle
a want, a need—a gypsy-mirrored skirt
twirling over scrub brush, desert rocks.

Desire. Not because I was the lone car
driving that stretch of road and she
appeared for me: pinpoint flecks
of sunlight, the twisting August wind,

flint chips, twigs swirling at her feet—
she was moving when I rolled into the valley
and kept on long after I'd gone.
What is desire, but a body's longing

for itself: a wish to dissolve without fear
into each cell, each particle of want,
to become this chaos of sunlight, of dust and wind
moving through a valley, for herself, alone.

Recurring

I am always searching
    for the right restaurant—the one
        serving cantaloupe soup

and crawfish. Always I lose
    the address. Always the thug
        on the corner—Michelin Man

down coat, pay phone glued
    to his ear—gives me a nod.
        The subway cavern smells

like engine grease. A woman yells
    out a brick tenement window
        at a man descending

the station stairs, his fedora brim
    angled away from her
        always. A stale coffee taste

in my mouth, donuts deep frying
    in a vat behind the wrong diner's
        plate glass. Fog paints gray lines

down concrete overpasses. Dawn
    never breaks the charcoal day.
        Always a yellow cab rankles

the loose manhole cover. Always
    the circus act takes to the streets.
        Today, I'm the woman in the top hat

juggling cleavers. Next week
    I'm the ballerina dressed as
        a marionette abandoning her strings.

Somewhere in a Box Marked Keep

I'm looking for the words again, in the dusty file box
marked *literary theory*, in the pistil of a red trumpet

flower. Frigidaire offers its sputter and hum, with
the neighbor's leaf blower playing contra-rhythm

as I tear up the house. The woman who lives in
my broom closet taps her foot and advises, *Remember*

when you had them last—a cornfield in Iowa, 1993;
a university soccer game, hot cider and October

rain. I think I left them at a rest stop on Interstate 80,
on the shelf above the soap dispenser, in the space

between *I want* and *I will*. Yesterday, I pulled open
a head of red leaf lettuce and found the word *chicory*

hiding in the center. I think I left them in that
apartment in the West Village, in a cupboard, behind

the recycling bin and the Clorox, in the wine box
with the rag rug, where the fat old cat used to sleep.

Narrative

October surf washes up details
from stories I've quit trying to plot—

a whole walnut shell bleached
white, its ridges filed smooth, the half-

dissolved lozenge of a brick, a goat
carcass decomposing on a nest

of sea grapes. What happened to you
along the way? is the question

you ask a changed friend, or a truck's
rear-view mirror cocked toward

your face. How red sea glass tumbled
into the shape of New Jersey, how

the dime-sized sand dollar, thin
as Eucharist, rode the summer tumult

to the beach—I have no answers
for now. My ex visits in the form

of a charcoal-colored gull landing
on a driftwood plank, autumn-red

beak. He lifts two wings. Nothing is
what it seems: the crab's lost leg

is a sprig of ice plant rusted orange,
the bleached clam shell is a plastic

milk bottle cap. What made me believe
I could predict my life, decipher

this code? A stone the size of my hand—
its granite surface etched by crooked

white lines—is not a map. A flock
of pipers' one-inch beaks stitch

crooked paths into wet sand. I'm done
searching for patterns. Today,

this trail ends at my planted feet.

When

I used to believe in signs:
    the ocean leaving something
        brittle and unbroken on the sand

for me to find, or the fog horn
    I heard from my dark bedroom
        after you told me to listen

hazy mornings before dawn,
    that low moan guiding minor
        vessels away from craggy

harm. If there were
    guarantees in love, then
        yes, I would follow you

to New York City, Puerto
    Rico, a place of birth, yours
        or mine. I used to believe in

tides pulling bodies toward
    unknown purples and deep,
        deep greens—that a dream

about blue whales signified
    desire, terrifying and good, rising
        in the body after a decade-long

fight. Back then I would track
    a barn swallow's crooked path
        across an August-drought field,

    expecting cattails and water
        to emerge from the earth,
            and they would. When I

believed in signs, a coyote
    pawing at dry brush, her tail
        a flag among weeds, told me

I should look for you,
    and a black-tailed deer
        holding my gaze meant:

if I could find you, you would stay.

Other Nights

A translucent spider
        eases its way down
                an invisible thread

I wouldn't see if light
        weren't cutting through
                a passing cloud at this

right instant. Sometimes
        I can't quiet the words
                in my head long enough

to hear clearly those
        uttered by anyone else.
                Not even love. Or hate.

Other nights, a light bulb
        falls from a bum socket
                ten miles away and I feel it

shattering on asphalt.
        Tell me again, great
                green leaf, black lizard

with white pinstripes
        and neon blue tail,
                what your name is,

and I will try, still pond
        absorbing sunlight,
                to remember this time.

If

> *Lovers don't finally*
> *meet somewhere. They're in*
> *each other all along.*
>
> Rumi

Then all I have to do is
recognize her, lifting

groceries from a cart into
the trunk of her car or

pulling a muddied garden glove
from her hand as I bike

slowly by. That
simple: a cherry branch

shimmers on puddled
water, and fire torches up

within, after so much rain.

Creature

It had the chrome-scaled body
of a sardine, pointed blue wings,

a barn swallow's, a sewer rat's
ringed tail and yellow teeth.

It coughed blue sparks, thrashed
in the ice plant as I stepped up

on the curb outside her house.
Hung from its neck, a dog tag

read: *Love.* Which explains why
I was scared to touch it, or walk away.

Q to the 6 Train

> *Desire is like that,*
> *pulling the lover to act and not act,*
> *again and again, pulling.*
>   Sophocles

The accordion player
    sits on an overturned
        milk crate, instrument

alive on her belly—
    black lacquered
        wood, opalescent

trim, pleated tapestry
    fanning and closing,
        her fingers working

chipped keys. Her waltz
    echoes off tiled station
        walls, and I know

I can stop this
    instant, move
        as music demands:

grab your small hand,
    spin your body
        like a dancer's,

pull your hips
    to meet mine,
        and kiss you. Or,

spend the rest of my life
       wishing I had—running
              from the Q to the 6 train,

metal wheels already clicking the tracks.

Getting It Right This Time

If we ever meet, wordless,
    staccato of December rain
        hammering the metal overhang,

may the person I am then
    press my tired hand to your
        rounded belly, trace a finger

around the equator I mapped
    our first night, orbiting
        from navel back to navel

to call you mine. If it ever
    happens like that, if some
        post-apocalyptic day we're made

strangers by too much buried
    pain, may the person you are then
        remember that hobos paint,

with their wet fingers, barely visible
    signs on dusty farmhouse doors.
        Remember an inverted triangle

with two dots above it says
    this one will give you water,
        two lines cut across an oval

means *this one will take you in.*

Dark Magic

From inside the black envelope
I slide a pressed lock of hair

onto my palm, shape of a comma,
small animal curled in sleep.

If these were silk threads
on the fabric store rack

the spool would rest between
burgundy and autumn brown.

You laughed when I warned
against sending hair—

material for voodoo, I said,
remembering the man

in New Orleans who brought
a paper sack to the barber,

swept his cut hair
from the checkered floor

and carried it home
for proper burial—*Never know*

when it could fall into the wrong hands,
he rasped. Foolish woman,

don't you know touching this
only makes me want more?

The hungry inside me
kick up their greed, light

the black candles, cast the spell—
I'm the night breeze pushing open

gauze curtains, the tangled curl
licking your bare breast, the wing-beat

pulse between your thighs.

Say Yes

The texture of tree bark beneath my hand
as I steady myself against the trunk,

hook my thumb in the heel of my shoe,
release my bare foot onto wet grass.

Naked—we become, not lovers glowing, but
dark of turned earth, questions

held on the tongue. Velvet of July's
humidity warms the skin as we cross

the dirt road to the pond—not inky, not
oil—water in a diviner's black bowl.

Step in, your hand says, sliding from
my neck to the hollow of my back.

Swamp grass, silt, mossy rock
slipping underfoot—I'll say yes

to anything—dark night, cool water
rising. You, coiling my thigh.

Gary Cooke

What I Remember

Photo by Karol Rice.

Gary Cooke's poems reflect his belief that the mysteries and wonders of life happen in particular moments, and that poems are photographs of those moments. Gary is a native of Canada who has lived most of his life in California — in the rich San Joaquin Valley, the spectacular central coast and the Sierra Nevada. He and his wife, artist Natalie Cooke, now make their home in Austin, Texas. His poems have appeared in literary journals and a chapbook, "Butterfish & Other Poems," published by The Heyeck Press. His work was also included in *Sierra Songs & Descants*, published by Hip Pocket Press in 2003.

After Seeing 'Edward Hopper, The Paris Years'

Three trees silhouetted
along the spine of a Sierra ridge;
his brush strokes of people hurrying
across *Le Pont des Arts*.
One bent, another twisted,
a third full-figured
and wearing a thick coat.

The slabs of shadowed gray
he called *Notre Dame*
are these monuments of stone
that nearly reach as high as thunder.

Across the pass, sunset's colors
are the golds and buttercreams
he saw against those light-struck walls.

Once, I saw a rolling flock of birds
above an empty field, moving
the way a gray whale
slides through heaving waves.

Art Show

for Natalie

All those paintings
radiant with light
none as bright with love
as her face,
turning in a crowd,
her soul in her eyes,
her heart's story
showing everything.
These are mine,
she is saying, these
are from my trip to France.
In a room of strangers
she is my one friend.
If I could paint her
anytime,
I would paint her now.

Backyard in Summer

In the hypnotized afternoon, bees come,
wings silky and legs powdered gold.
Yarrow trembles as low breezes hunt
the ground. Sweet peas and night blooming jasmine
reach up, catnip and roses, gladiola on long stalks,
clay pots of pansies. All the flowers naked,
spread like sluts in the yellow light.

The sun rubs itself across the sky. A woman dreaming,
rolling in her bed, her mind delicious, her fingers
digging in hot dirt. Crepe myrtle, status, bougainvillea, veronica,
dark reds and purples swollen. The throats of hummingbirds
glittering in the light. Sweet smells, tomatoes hanging
behind leaves, a bell pepper begging for a tongue.

Grass softens, a whole yard dreaming of sex,
the warm wind making everything want touching.

Biting at the Rain

The sudden storm
made music on the water,
wind swaying reeds
along the shore.

I turned my canoe
toward a cove and stroked,
while fish leaped, flying high,
biting at the shining rain.

The Big Blue Ball

I don't know what it meant
when the man held the big blue ball
at the end of his driveway,
swilling a beer, and swaying,
while the two children
waited near the garage door.
I just saw it when I drove by,
and when I looked in the mirror,
he was still standing there,
holding the big blue ball
like maybe it was something bigger
than that, and waiting, I guess,
for the two kids to know
whatever the hell he wanted them to know
before he'd throw it.

Bits of Glass

It was this beach
where I collected
bits of rounded,
colored glass,
put them in a shell
and left them
at the door of a woman.
The nights she held me
are like that, rounded
by the years
into imperfect memories,
a treasure to keep
in the deepest colors
of my mind, the ocean
still rolling in and out,
the years piling up
like sand.

Dead Poem

If I write
one more great
blue heron poem,
I'm going to
kill it.

How many ways
can it lift
above the water
and glide away
or gather
the silence
with its wings,
and call its rattle
to the other shore?

Its shadow
always ripples
like evil
on the waves,
and my heart beats
slightly faster.

It sees me
with its button eyes
and spreads feathers
like the winter wind.

It hides along
the river's edge,
dreaming dark shapes
in the water.

I think of dying
by a sharp stick.
I think of death.

Bang.

The Curve of Earth

Memories walk like deer
through the fields, stepping
carefully in the dusk.

Butterflies hang in eucalyptus
trees, all the poems and hopes
that hiked along dirt roads.

In the waving grass,
the sun still sets the poppies
aflame with all those kisses.

Prayers lift like gulls
above the sea, spiral in the wind,
fly higher, and disappear.

The spray blows hard
across the mouth of the river,
tears stinging in orange sunsets.

Or fog darkens the sky
to gray, gathering like unknowns
and hiding the winding road home.

All those hours sitting on stones,
or lying on slopes of rolling hills,
come back to me like waves against the shore.

Didn't I live here, and die
a hundred times, gazing at the curve of earth,
wishing I could find my way?

Ducks Leaving

When the ducks rise
on the far bank
you first see glitter,
the sun exploding
in a splash of water,
until the birds
are in the air—
a slapping of wings
that takes an afternoon
by surprise. They fly
in straight, rising lines
until some ancient tuning
makes them slant away,
circle slowly, their thin souls
eager in the wind, and
point upriver until they are gone.
You watch the light
sliding on the river.
A year might be going by,
the glitter gone, but your heart
still pumping like wings
above the wind.

Flying Fox

Some animal
left a rope of shit
on the trail,
no tracks or other sign.
I think it must have been a fox
that dropped it,
while in a great leap,
silhouetted on a low moon,
who hurried home
to exclaim his prowess.
I've learned to shit while flying,
he cried.
Mother Fox kept stirring
at her pot.
Father Fox, looking up
from his New Yorker,
said, Well done, son.
That will be a good thing to know
someday.

King of the Rooftop

I envy the goat down the road
that spends most days mounted

on the roof of the doghouse
in his littered yard, aware of nothing

but his hunger, and the endless supply
of cans tossed on the lawn by the owner.

And star thistle for dessert. Goats don't
question anything, or get upset by politics.

They don't pretend to be nice,
or not to smell like themselves.

Sure, a chain hangs from his neck,
but who's not caught in some web,

despite all efforts to seem free?
Better to be king of your own rooftop

in a domain of rusting trucks
than to live life in the dark rooms

of a mortgaged house, never knowing
the world in black and white,

or the clatter of your crown of horns
when you ram bang against life,

the wind in your balls, your cock swinging
like a billy club on the meanest street in town.

Koi Pond

In their dark pond
they glide, ancient spirits
in bright robes, moving
with flicks of their sleeves.

They are breathing gods
who move toward us, then away,
when they know we have
nothing to give.

The afternoon sun
makes the surface seem clear,
but they disappear, slipping
beyond the world we see.

The Question

My father died slowly,
his life a question mark
of old shoulders
and bent knees.

One day he napped
on my bed
until he could coax
his legs to move.

I rested my head
in the mark he'd left
on my pillow,
my arms still shaped
by our hug.

At the end he suddenly
lifted himself to look around,
but we never knew
if he saw us,
or anything at all.

Red Moon

Her mouth was a kiss
waiting to change my life.
When we parted,
her face glowing
like a pearl
in the dark night
of my dreaming,
I saw the crescent
of a red moon
tilting over the city,
as though she had pressed her lips
on the memory
of our moment.

The Road Between Them

This kind of country
makes your heart spill.
Wildflowers everywhere,
a sign saying
Sweet Medicine Ranch.

Just below Latrobe
the dark eyes of a mare
disturb you, until the curve
in the road lets you see the horse
on the other side, head down
in the long grass.

The road between them
wet and dark, a sky purple
with thunder, you feel something like love,
even driving by,
big drops of rain splashing
like tears on the windshield.

This Part of Texas

Squalor is a plastic bag
shredding in the thorns
of a wire fence, trees
blown bare by winter.

In this part of Texas
winter is a whiskery thing,
the face of an old cowboy
too long in the hard light.

You can see the pain
of dry earth, the way cows
kick dust as they search
the barren fields for grass.

In the dirt yards
dogs watch trucks go by
while grey sheds lean
and play sets stand empty.

You wonder what a woman thinks
as she stands, her hair blowing,
arms folded beneath her breasts,
lips as thin as the horizon.

She turns and climbs
the trailer stairs in her blue dress,
the whole sky pressing down
and no way to change the wind.

What I remember

is the pale form
behind the trees
as twilight came
the moon bouncing
as I drove descending
through the hills
uncertain
if I'd seen a horse at all
or the spirit of a horse
or the moon
tossing its head
in the field
another restless night
under a sky too big
the grass dark
and the water
in the nearby pond
even darker.

The Windows

What if the windows
in all the hotels in Reno
are really the eyes of wolves,
dead from guns or bad winters,
and their tails are the winds
that sweep across the valley?

And every time a woman gets kissed,
the wolves are licking their lips?
What if great jaws snap and drool
when a woman flips her hair,
or a man drops his cigarette
and turns away?

What if all these eyes are waiting
for one wolf to move,
his huge paws spreading
as he trots in closing circles,
and night howls in aching sadness
the way every train sounds,
winding down the mountain
and hauling toward the city,
the red neon pulsing,
the lights burning all the windows bright?

Your Smile

I like your smile
because it's so
uncomplicated.

My own face sometimes
is a horror of
good intentions.
I feel like a bad picture
of myself.

I'd like to take your face
with its smile
and skip it like a flat stone
across some jingling river,
and turn around
and love myself.

Judy Halebsky

Lay It Down

With a dedication to writing as the work of a community and as part of a dialogue, Judy Halebsky often works in collaboration with dancers and musicians and participates in writing workshops. Her poems have been published in *Five Fingers Review, Grain Magazine* and *Rattlesnake Review*. The issues of translation in her work and her visual poetry reflect her time studying calligraphy at the Kanazawa College of Art in Japan on a research fellowship. The MacDowell Colony, the Millay Colony, and the Canada Council for the Arts have supported her work. Originally from Halifax, Nova Scotia, she now lives in Sacramento.

Lay it down

There were people in restaurants, there were bars and cigarettes
there were summer nights in parks where the lamplight made shadows
    over the trees
and people were kissing and summer dresses were thin
there were people who went to concerts and danced in high heeled
    shoes who groped
strangers who drank too much who woke up in the morning and had
    coffee with cream
and crepes and told outrageous stories of the night before

                                                      that wasn't me

I was looking in the windows, leaning weak against the doorframe,
    restless, swollen
aching my hips unsettled
there were doctors in lab coats doctors with nice houses and cars
there were doctors with tests with theories
doctors with crystals and mood rings
there were ladies on Oprah there were strangers on the street
saying try aloe vera, vitamin B, shark fin, gingerroot

I was burnt flat out but then there was fireweed, and moss and ferns
    again and after that
there were parties to go to with cosmopolitans and Cuban bands and
    tight dresses and
night air and the grip of a man learning to dance
coming out of it now, everything is better than I thought
the high notes, the driveway kisses, the ice cream

I was sick, I looked terrible Felt aweful i was broken down to losing
 everyday was worse
so i started to let go to clean out old closets, put my shoe box of regrets
 out with trash, i
had to loosen up my dreams,
i had to clean out old closets, i had to loosen up dreams, i had to not
 care about the
places i'd left, i had to pull myself back into the living, from a burned
 out forest

i made myself a burned out forest, where everything was lost when all
 the tragedy and
dissapointment and the pressure of failing was gone i laid and rested
 then i could rest,
then i was read y to go to give up but the fire weed came first and the
 moss and the ferns.
clear the way for the fireweed the moss the low lying greens

i dried out like a burned field scorched and barren then i clean out old
 closets, loosened
up on my dreams, i had to not care about the places i'd left, i had to lay
 out with nothing
behind me and nothing before me
somehow

there was my sixteen year old car there was me with a part time job my
 room in a
boarding house, my family far and further away and the sickness it was
 growing
i was stretchd too thin too many things lost and longing

62

i had to lose everything and then like a forest after the fire slowing
  growing back

burned out and still

like i'd never done it before, like coming up over the edge and jumping
to the tired, exhusted from a night of parties and talking rather than
  from sleepless hours
upon hours

nothing helped
the lady on opera had a different problem but one days she was better
  just like walking
out of a dark tunnel into light she said and I hoped that was me
she said you had to want to be get better
but me I was stripped and bare, something inside me has tear
inside I was dried out like march after the snow when everthing has
  been ded and frozen
for months and I was walking across the frozen marsh with that clear
  blue winter sky and
those old man bare trees walking cautious over the ice i had fallen
  through over the ice i
had use my mittens to pull out off over the burning just before freezing i
  was walking
away

i
and there were people through windows
talking on phones
there were people complaining about the service
there were people spending days in shopping malls
there were people sleeping all day
three was me in boat on the river with the current and the storm

laid out flat watching the sky there was the hum of rapids
there was breaking and the spray

it wasn't like coming out of a dark tunnel
it was more like walking on the ice
and I said oh, look at the sky clear blue of winter
look that the bare old man branches
look at this lake stretching on forever
look at me walking here where once i fell through

nothing helped i got worse and worse

i would collect straws, i would fumble with coins i would drive home
    and cry
i was drying out i was empiting all the greens i'd known all the good
    days were from
sometime when i didn't know it would end or that i'd forget how much
    i'd wanted to live

i counted elements water rice air
my bones emtied I ate broth on opera they said you had to want to get
    better
and i i did but there was the hopelessness, the sickness

i was laid out rock drying and brittle

and then there was the lady on opera who didn't go outside for seven
    years and then she
mustered up her will and thought about outside and inside and fear and
    what she might be
missing like ice cream sundaes on the patio or walking in the spary of a
    fountain or plum
blossems that lighting through the air across lawns over cars, sidewalks
    and porches,
plum blossoms the first in spring
and she said when she finally went out it was like coming out of a dark
    tunnel
and maybe this could be my time of darkness and maybe some I too
    could emerge

it's not quit like stepping outside
I still like in the glass the house
with the weak bones
the fragile
the lost days into years

resurfacing wanting to go back to live over all the days I lost all my
    regret to redue but
pass this let this on do these things today

there were days i wanted like that

お空はちょっとも飛べない
Oh sky, a little bit even, fly not

You can move between French and English
put the table in the kitchen
and the soft red chair by the window

but with Japanese you can't bring what you already have
like the words: me, you
or how to count: 1 bed, 2 chairs, 3 days

an airplane takes off from Sacramento
I lie at an angle so I can see the fig tree out the window

arms for wings
ears for songs
3 days for water
sleep for sleep
chocolate for chocolate
vodka for vodka
kanji for death
death for surrender
surrender for sleep and 10,000 years

the sky is (o for honorific)
a little bit (silent syllable) even
I (implied) cannot fly

I cannot fly in the sky at all

楚 Woman Under Trees

suede sneakers and bay windows
you would find me
a couple bars under healthy
in the bedroom too small
with all the noise from the street

it's the harvest Mom says
work night and day
so there'll be food in the winter
she's talking about me and homework
and trying to graduate

you might think these aren't my words
not my body, not sounds that shaped me
when I was growing through shadows on the wall

> 海女 *amame*
>> ocean woman:
>> a woman diving for shells

> 姦 *kan*
>> three women:
>> wickedness and mischief

> 雨女 *ameonna*
>> rain woman:
>> a woman who brings rain

these words flood into the river
they are trees that rise uprooted
they are butterflies in the trees

My Father Remembers Blue Zebras

He remembers that he lost his wallet

he knows about the rainshadow
and the string of islands off the coast of Vancouver

      覚える
         oboeru   to remember
                        also means to learn

I try to keep track of what he put where
the small green car we called Cricket
the second time he got drafted
and Aunt Nina's husband, *he's a nice guy but he's a fascist*

he's asking me again
where do you live
oh, you're in school, what do you study

how far off coast do you have to go
to be sheltered from the rain

that's wonderful Dad says, *that's wonderful*

Thinned by Storm

You might think that *kamikaze* means suicide pilot
but really it's a way of not saying something
a way of counting what's missing

> *Kami* — god
> *Kaze* — wind
> Divine wind
> God of the wind
> God of the trees

I'm counting on my fingers
on my toes
tracing the patterns on my skin
the blood lines, the needles, the nurses

worse than this the man on the radio says
is to be a parent to someone equally wounded

to my mother, I hand over the long nights
in pounds of salt, in gray canvas, in folded sheets

my swollen joints, layers of chalk skin
veins withered, leaves in the frost

I should protect her
I should tell her it doesn't hurt at all

instead I keep her with me
we walk in the late afternoon leaves
maple
elm
fall around us

Whale Music

I.

There are paper maps of fishing routes
the gulf stream, the whale surfacing areas

you make a map of the days in between

these are numbers you need for the map:
68, 63, 60, 56, 42, 40, 50

then you'll need a string tied to a nail
now you can make lines, measure distance, think about proportions

like how much water there is in the ocean
how many fish there used to be
and how big a whale is compared to a human body

these are the words you need for the map:
Atlantic cod, fishing rights, gully, bank, 100 fathoms

Roseway, La Have, Canso
Sydney Island
St. Johns
Hamilton Inlet

fathom: to determine the depth of sound
fathom: to find the nature of
fathom: to measure the depth of the ocean

II.

Fish houses, coast guard, longitude
they surface now and then
out the window down the bay we can see
a dark shiny stretch coming up in the water

mica straining whale music, lobster traps, sardines

we'll walk out and watch from far away
we'll spend a few hours or the whole afternoon
watching the whales breathe

mica straining, lobster traps, sardines

lawn fertilizers drain into the ocean
collect in their blubber
in their kidneys and liver
as they're straining fish through their horse hair teeth
pulling in mica and cod and sea weed

fathom: to measure the depth of the ocean
fathom: to determine the nature of
fathom: to hear the sound of whales

III.

Late August out on the porch in Lunenburg
laughing, drinking, beer bottles and cheese bread

draw a line across the page
this is the ground

whale music — that's what he called it
the man who made music to summon the whales

re-trace the line across the page
this is the sky

draw a small line at an angle
this is the coastline
it goes into the ocean
the ocean goes

fathom: callused hands pulling in nets
fathom: to know the nature of
fathom: to measure loss

On the Coast

I forget how to measure with my hands
the length between the root cellar
the room at the back of the house
the clothesline and the shore

I forget the dream fish, the tooth fairies
the angel's wings on me in the night

I forget how to nestle the worry
up into my lungs
tuck my memories into the dark crevasses
with the tobacco and stale smoke

how I moved so far away, why I didn't study biology
where were the babies when these weary bones could stay up all
night

I try to remember
to feel the dry texture of breadfruit in my mouth
the sand shifting into the shape of my body
our shadows in the night while I push you to push me
out into the water
that lasts forever
and then disappears

Landscape

to Jessie LeBaron

Hang me, your honor, up with the furniture
the dictionary is out of words, out of pages

let me sleep with the shadows on the north face
let me sleep with the limestone, sleep with the ash
sleep with the winged insects captured there

let me dream the blank pages that were once a dictionary
let me run my fingers over the smooth Braille
let the images of each entry evaporate
into pockets of air of sleep of denim

the water is moving underground
there are so many of us and each desperate

I should go to Oakland
where no one has what they need
search the corners between Fruitvale and MacArthur
between High Street and 73rd
for paper cups, taco shells, tootsie roll comic strips

in Japanese there's a character that means searching for something
and a different character
that means searching for something you've lost

I open the dictionary again, still blank

The Big School

Daddy uses big words
because no one understands
he failed kindergarten with glasses and earaches
and Fanny shouting into the phone
who fails kindergarten?

he learned English like a math test
with a thousand variables
calculations, equations, limitless permutations

Maya wants to go to college
so she's learning words out of a book for the test
pedantic — using really big words for no reason
tortuous — extra super complicated
cloyed — to eat so much chocolate you just can't eat any more

she says she's heard them all before from Daddy
but she never knew what he meant
about her insipid pop music
her Friday night mendacity
her teenage ennui

Monster Walking in a Snowstorm with Feet Tied Together (a painting)

Mr. Spencer met my dad
and he's still laughing
saying *you're your daddy's girl
your daddy's girl*
shakes his head and laughs

and I just know Daddy came in all excited
and talked and talked and talked
loud like New York and everyone else
froze still, stood back and stared
but he doesn't notice
just keeps right on
about what is terrible and wonderful
warm and desolate

Mr. Spencer can't believe it either
*what does your dad do
when did he move here*

Daddy comes to get me after school
sees Mr. Spencer and my painting

Daddy thinks it's really something special
he keeps asking Mr. Spencer what he thinks
if he can see it too, the special something about it
the blue snow or monster feet
Mr. Spencer smiling wide and nodding

Mr. Spencer says, *your dad,* and smiles real big
your dad, and laughs

Daddy says he teaches people about people
but that's not really the word
I want to know the word
so when people ask me what he does
I can tell them

He won't tell me because I don't know
he thinks I won't understand
but I just want to know the word
so I can tell other people
like passing along a note I won't read
or a cup of water I won't spill

Purcell's Cove Road

if I were to say, our house collapsed in the
storm, if I were to say, the china was in
pieces, if I were to say, Daddy's voice still
echoes, even without the walls

        you would know

that I sat days on the doorstep waiting for
him, that there aren't hurricanes in Nova
Scotia, that he didn't take everything with
him, but he tried

(notes on why)

they were trying to make a bomb
and they had this guy Heisenberg
who understood uncertainty and particles
and the chances of what would move where

this was after relativity
where light bends around a door
and things that seem to happen at the exact same time
actually happen at different times

Nagasaki depends on the angle
on how you measure
Manchuria, soldiers, civilians and God

dear Jessie, I'm trying to calculate the chances

measure him out in probability
but it's not looking good
there's an infinite number of things that can happen
and no one knows why out of all the options
only one gets pinned down into the present moment

and on top of that
being together at the same space in time and location
depends on where you're looking from

and it gets worse
because time changes with how fast you travel
so you might feel like it was just a week ago
but the same week for him could be three years
and by now he's woken up without you
almost a thousand times

Red Hollow

I mark days in lines on the bedpost
bathe in salt water and ice cream

please don't tell anyone about the salt
or the midnight radio
or the patterns in my blood

I believe in skiing over the rocks when the snow is thin

when my mother got cancer she said
the goal now is to die of something else

I'd be better off with faith

My father is calling Karl Marx a prophet

we danced our feet crunching in back yard snow

getting better is something to say
instead of grave or progressive

I believe in throwing all my dresses off the roof

we are sword fighting in shadows on the wall
we are walking through the woods with wet mittens
we are reading the sign by the lake that says the ice will hold

Down the Mountain

Take me as nothing left
lift me twisted through granite and moss
water lung, milk waist, sage
I pass through these pages like a ghost

erase my shape in the sun on the porch
brown my skin into the riverbed
push my words into a lullaby
paper lung
milk waist and sage
whatever I came with exhausted
I pass through these pages like a ghost
whatever I came with I spent

Scott V. Young

The Language of Longing

Scott V. Young is a part time teacher, poet and actor, appearing in *Corpse* with the Foothill Theatre Company and *Glengarry Glen Ross* at the Northern California Center for the Arts. He did graduate work in creative writing at San Francisco State University where he co-founded *Ink*, an independent publication of creative expression. A former journalist and bookseller, his writing has appeared in *Publisher's Weekly*, the *American Bookseller's Association* magazine, San Francisco *Bay Guardian*, the Santa Cruz *Good Times* and the *San Francisco Independent* as well as in smaller publications over the years. Along with his three delightful children, he lives in an unfinished house by a creek in the country just north of Nevada City, California, where he gardens a little and sometimes stops to look at birds.

The Language of Longing

for Jaime

Speaking the language of longing and distance,
the wild gabble of horizons gilded by a sun
that always sinks but never seems to set,
they circle above in the nearly translucent blue air,
so thin and clear today I swear you can see endless emptiness
just outside the bent and thinning branches at the roof of the sky.

These are the Sandhill cranes again,
visitors from some other land come to deliver
an invitation, a warning, a solicitation,
ceaseless as the sea in their circling,
in their long thin lines,
their motionless glide.

I stand amidst the creeping sadness of late September
old lusts resurrected by their cry,
dry dust running like sweat beneath my skin,
each fall's autumnal fade awakening antique grief.

Of course they know, those who wander in the bottomless sky.
They know of long days lost, unspoken.
They too see that endless empty space above.

Too soon wings roll away, away
called to the west by promises vaguely felt.
And I remain, caressing the skin of the incessant soil
held by the earth, the slow language of oaks, whisperings of grasses.

In a moment I turn to your question across the silent air
to your smile, to the angle of your lips.

I turn and turn like a dervish in prayer
your sun the source of each revolution

your eyes the reason.

Winter Morning Walk

Just before dawn, the cold and the dark weave together
into something thicker than either.
Like glass which becomes water the moment it is touched,
the night opens as I pass through, then closes behind me,
eddies of disturbed air whirlpooling beneath an absence of moon.

I cannot see my feet on the gravel road
so seek light in the strangely dim stars,
thousands of them, one in every direction
yet still not bright enough to matter much,
nothing more than pretty baubles
lightly gilding the curving blackness above.
Their shallow glitter does not beckon me tonight,
promises nothing. They are mute witnesses waiting for dawn
when one thing hesitates to leave and another
to arrive.

The darkness lingers a moment longer than it should
and in a few steps I know the reason why.
Unable to see, instead I hear the little creek
long before I cross it and hear, in an instant,
the question it carries, has always carried:
What is the sound of water hitting water,
the sound of curves carved in air,
stones and surfaces and falling and echoes
rushing toward one ear and away
from the other, out of quiet and into quiet,
what we call silence but which is not empty
and is not silent?

Why I Climb Mountains

Like everything else I do
it starts with the urge to hurry,
my journey up the slope like panic,
like a five year old wanting to be first in line.
Slivers of view soon unfold, tantalize,
generate more momentum so that
I cannot stop climbing and race forward,
take risks, even stumble foolishly
addicted to distance and seeing,
to seven layers of hills in the dancing air,
torn paper strips, tints of absence,
the edge of the world out there, somewhere.

At the top I sit cross-legged in sharpened air
perched on a strip of granite no wider than my knees
far above a lake so blue it shames the sky.
For a moment I believe
I could as easily fly as fall.

Above, the house of the clouds beckons
but the path to it is hidden to me still.
Instead I watch as they birth and unbirth,
surge, dip, swirl and render themselves anew,
like the water they are and
the air they so long to be.

In seconds I succumb to the anonymous wilderness,
another place I've never been, another empty piece of the earth.
I become stone to long uncaring whips of cold, stone to
a wailing river flowing over the top of the world,
but stone with ears to hear this wind's relentless keen
from the death bed barrows of ancient kings,
blown across ages and oceans,
over continents and battlefields,
orchards with fruit that will never ripen,
waves breaking in the middle of the sea.
If I wait long enough I become the wind, too,
condemned to carry the sound of longing
if longing sounded like grief
and grief sounded like nothing at all,

like ten thousand miles of nothing
with ten thousand more to go.

The Heron

The heron walks with meticulous care
as if each step mattered more
than the one before, each
infinitesimal shift of flesh and feather
a mere illusion.

Even the water that drips from his toes
appears to fall toward Earth
with more than usual caution,
seeming to pass through the surface of the pond
to the depths unhindered,
each ripple fading before it begins.

Perhaps if he sets down his foot more softly,
closes his eyes,
waits for the wind to fade,
he will one day find
the water bears his weight.

And what will we do then?

Will we hold our breath
watch the world flicker
and grow still—
the thin air full of silent premonition?

My Cat Asks a Question

It's 5am.
A storm unfolds beyond the bedroom windows,
steady flow of darkened clouds delaying dawn,
rattling gusts of frustrated rain against the glass.
Noises cease when the wind settles down,
like the steady breathing of the deepest sleeper.
In the silences between breaths
there is a promise or two I'm counting on:
The phone will not ring, children will not waken,
I will drift back and forth on the shore,
caught in the waves mixing story and dream.
I have an hour to incubate,
to bathe in daylight's lazy ease.

Downstairs, my cat asks a question.
Mrow?
Bastard, I think,
then quiet even my thinking in hopes
he'll go away.

But it's too late. He knows where I am,
knows where I sleep.
Mrow? he says, a resonant inquiry, and
mrow? again. He is coming up the stairs,
three or four steps, then mrow? then more steps.

Just outside my door he sits on his fat haunches,
comfortably wrapped in semi-darkness,
all the time in the world. Every 20 seconds
he asks again, mrow? his voice rising in perfect inflection,
content to wait forever, posing his eternal question.

It's 5am, he says.
Do you know where your cat is?

Restless Invitation

My girls float away from me laughing
two dark dots growing smaller
caught by choice in the lazy September river
in the insistent pull of water over
stone and stone over water
trapped in the sticky honey of beckoning light,
golden spokes of late afternoon in the mountains
when shadows slide noiselessly down the face of distant slopes
and fish kiss endless circles into surfaces.

I remain behind, squinting down river and into my past
at years of days spent watching every
flashing sun that ever dipped into the ocean,
every strip of liquid fire cast carelessly before me,
mute and restless invitation
to attend, to follow,
shed my shirt and skin and
enter the burning sea,
walk a path of shifting light
to the west, always to the west,
a thousand miles or a thousand days,
until sea becomes sky
where I must stop

        and watch them
even smaller now, a hand or a hint of laughter
rising up, against the purple twilight,
against the new born stars.

"The Pumpkin Knew Too Much"

Title of a Halloween drawing by Alex, age 6

You could tell by the crooked grimace
on his puffy orange face
by the anxious flickering in his eyes.

Last night he had enjoyed himself
clustered on the kitchen table
with other pumpkins
lights and laughter.
He had lost his usual reserve,
come out of his shell
so to speak.
He got it. Halloween and all.

It was different now.
Darker, somehow.
People tromped by, one after another,
like robots or zombies
intent on one thing.
Mechanical.

He spent the night
looking at shoes,
feeling empty.

'This is the end of something'
he thought.

The Kiss

The full moon rises flat and fast
a misshapen bubble of golden grease
popping up from the black shape of hills
into a night sky so clear only an instant
passes before the gold is gone,
and in its place a clean silver circle waits,
an incandescent dragonfly hovering
over a pond as wide as the northern hills,
intent for one moment
on not making the next move,
on not being the instant
before or after.

Startled by the sudden arrival
of so much silent light
deer in a nearby meadow quicken,
then still, one ear forward or back.
The candle on the table between us
flickers once, caught between flame
and darkness, between heat and hesitation.

In your eyes is an arrow drawn back tight
by an archer who holds her breath,
waiting for the string to slip away,
for the moon to make a move,
for the touch of wing to water.

Late Night Violin Practice with Margarita

I have recently taken up violin
and margaritas, though
not necessarily in that order.

It begins with lime, salt and
enough tequila to feel it in your nose
when you exhale,

enough lime to make you pucker up
a bit, and salt to make you thirsty
so you'll take another sip.

This paves the way for Lesson 1:
Twinkle Twinkle Little Star
written by Mozart when he was just 3

and the first song taught
on every instrument I've ever played.
A song I must have heard a thousand times.

More. But, until now, never understood,
or even liked. Taste the lime, exhale,
play it again. It's nice. Melodic. Just six notes.

Same six notes in *Go Tell Aunt Rhody*,
which is Lesson 3. Only two strings so far.
'Why,' my daughter asked earlier, her head tilted sideways

to hold the violin on her thin shoulder,
'why does Aunt Rhody want to know?'
Myself, I always thought she loved the old goose

and wanted to mourn it, but perhaps,
my daughter opined, she simply wanted to eat it.
A quandary. Another sip. Another.

Lesson 7: *Long Long Ago*, seven notes. Coincidence?
I think not. Even more momentous—the third string.
Complexity, resonance, possibility. Judicious swallow.

All are in bed and night enfolds the house.
Lesson 9: *Perpetual Motion*—My life:
It ends and there is silence

it begins and there is music and
somewhere in between
drinking.

Imagined Anniversary

for my father

Though I know which day you were born
and which day you died
(the phone call from the hospital,
my mother, your new widow
hanging on to the phone with both hands,
her sobs shattering our breakfast chatter)
neither day has since become a reckoning;
celebrated, dreaded or assigned certain powers.

Instead, one year, I counted the days,
month by month, birth to death,
and marked a private anniversary
on my calendar: December 18th, 1997.
The first day I was older than you ever would be.

Like the eldest son in a fairytale forest,
seeking the father who went away one day,
and never came back, I wished that I could
enter the myth of memory to find you again.
We would smoke a cigar on one of the piers, watching ships,
get a haircut at Red's Place, beers at a bar you knew
run by an old buddy from the Navy,
steak and martinis at a strip club over on Broadway.
It would be '68, of course. We'd wear hats and ties,
the air would be crisp. We'd be 36, and alive.

Now, each day I'm a little older than you ever were,
and each December a whole year passes
filled with phone calls I never made,
mistakes you avoided the hard way,
goodbyes tossed away as carelessly as hellos.

You are forever a young man with a handful of children
fighting a battle you will never win,
full of punch and bravado, dreaming of something big.
And I, graying in my beard,
forever a child, hair neatly parted,
slicked down, attending second grade
and learning the days of the week.

I Love My Penis

The front of my new shiny black refrigerator
(itself the essence of sophisticated absence)
is sparse and elegant, free of Christmas photos
or grocery lists with apple sauce underlined three times.
Instead it features just one magnet.
Oh, but what a magnet.
A gift from my wife and three young children
who know me all too well,
it says, in bold black letters on a white background

I Love My Penis

Of course, Love is symbolized by
the ubiquitous red heart.
This message was also intended for
my three year old son
who really does love his penis.

I mean, really.

He holds his penis like a comfort object,
a little pink teddy bear at exactly arm's length,
takes it with him everywhere he goes,
whispers endearments to it
and listens carefully to its responses.
If he could kiss his penis good night
he would.
Each night, he would pull it to his cheek gently,
like the shiny satin edge of his blanket
close his eyes and cuddle it
then sink in liquid sleep
lips just brushing
its blushing little tip.

Forsythia

It is spring, or nearly.
During my morning showers these last few weeks
I've watched the sun crest distant hills a little earlier
a little further north. Angled rays of light now
find my bathroom window easily,
turning water into veins of gold
that follow the curves of my flesh.

On the land the manzanita is in flower,
regular lines of pink and white, the air around them
awash with the scent of honey, heavy and golden,
so thick my hands come up as if to part a curtain
and I close my eyes—want no other distractions.

Like the chanting frogs each evening going silent as I approach,
or the smell of warmth arising from the earth itself,
it is enough just to know you're out there, somewhere
naked in the lilac-scented darkness,
wrapped in forsythia blossoms and stolen kisses.
It is enough to know I had you once.

Two owls emerge from winter's silence,
one in the tree by the window, the second down in the gully.
They talk all night, a slow rhythm,
each listening carefully for the other's reply,
discussing mice, I suppose, or negotiating terms.

Of love or surrender, I cannot say.

A Mother's Death

for Taylor

This morning I gave you the phone
so the voice on the other end could tell you to sit down,
could say what shouldn't have to be said to any 12-year-old.

Now we drive to the airport to take you home,
the road weaving in and out
between the lake's abrupt beginning
and the mountain's sudden end.
Long ropes of rain on the glass fall thick
then thin, then stop altogether,
just wipers still ticking a reluctant heartbeat
silence   echo   silence.

No longer only your teacher,
I circle my arms about you as if I could cage in your sorrow.
There is nothing to say, and there is too much to say.
Remember this day, I whisper, pointing through the wet glass.
The way the rain makes crossing ripples on the lake,
deep green trees and the darkness underneath.
The mist, I say, look at the white mist on the black mountains. It's alive.
I point again. Only your eyes move, slowly climbing the peak.

I am insistent: See how the ridges grow lighter as they reach higher?
How the dark slopes become indistinct, become cloud,
become shadow, then light itself?
You're going to need these memories.
For the rest of your life you'll come back to them.

The dogwood in flower, a scatter of
white blossoms beneath the pines
will never go away.
Memorize it, wreathed in maple green,
in madrone and birch and silver rain;
you will come back to it every day.

Through all my whispered words you remain silent,
do not speak for another hour or two,
and then only one line: Can't they save her?
A raw and broken prayer,
cast to the wind, already unanswered.

We both know it's a plea for resurrection,
for the earth to cease whirling,
or time to turn back, just once,
and fix this foolish mistake.

I wonder now:
Can you still remember the child's yellow chair
set out beside the road, empty but waiting
for someone who needed to sit down
who needed to rest?

Can you still see that abandoned grey house
collapsing into moss and cedar,
brambles rising up on all sides to protect it,
to shelter its long sleep?

Dusk and Silence

Why sit before this humming screen
or little yellow pad, alone, always,
early in the morning or
late in the afternoon,
surrounded anyway by changing light,
by the breathing in and out of the day,
slowly opening and closing my hand
as if one time I might find
a long lost silver coin?

What is it about the full moon
or the new, for that matter,
that needs describing one more time?
Hasn't love been dissected enough,
cut into strips like venison
then dried and chewed,
and chewed and chewed
or forgotten?

Aren't we all tired of writing
the word limn?
Or luminescent? Or epiphany?

Why then do I sit in this empty room
each surface limned with dying light,
with the swiftly fading luminescence
of yet another day?

Why do I hold my breath,
close my eyes,
lean in toward the screen
as if I could hear a heart beat
beneath the dusk and silence?

Cold

The dog ambles forward on the gravel path
more like a bear now that she's old
and fat. There's no spring in her step.

Even slower, I follow her, felled
by the flu and a lonely divorce,
making my way up the steep hill
beneath a tarnished bronze sky,
a winter sky.

I am cold, have been cold for days.
Even the startling flash of blue wings in the barren oak,
the brave little russet chests of bluebirds
brings me no particular joy.
I cannot shake any beauty from the landscape
no matter how hard I try.

I don't try that hard. I feel
like I'm done with trying for a while.

I grow old, Eliot on an empty beach
wondering about mermaids.

I'm done with mermaids, too.

And the bluebirds make me happy
no matter what I said.

Kirsten Casey

Everyone Else

Kirsten Casey's accomplishments include aspiring to be a professional roller skater and choreographing complex routines in her driveway; planning, and then giving up, on becoming a graphic designer when she found out it involved math; actually designing a book cover for a recent published novel; living in England for six months on Virginia Woolf's street; earning a Master's degree in Creative Writing from San Francisco State; giving birth to a 10-pound baby; and teaching poetry to sixth graders through the California Poets in the Schools program. She can be found at the kitchen sink in conversation with her husband or behind the wheel chauffeuring her three children to various activities. Sometimes she has a minute to write a poem.

Bad Girl

She leaves the dance early,
straddles the bleachers
in Wrangler jeans
she had to lie down to pull on,
the pockets pushed down
with a wooden-handled ice pick.

She pulls a boy behind her,
as if he were a blindfolded hostage.
Her stride is always forward—
those pointed boot tips,
her stamped silver name, spelled on her belt,
the closest thing she could get to a tattoo,
at sixteen.

The rest was left up to us:
what we knew or heard,
what we guessed and created.
The issue of the small flask,
how the backseat vinyl squeaked
beneath them, how she ever managed
to take off those jeans and put them on again.

She came back to the dance
at eleven p.m.,
waited for her mother
in the school parking lot,
like any other girl,
flushed from dancing,
wanting to keep a secret.

Maxine remembers the goats

Once she had been able to tell time
by the tone of their bleating.
Five goats in a pen, siblings, bought for her
to be raised for 4-H. As kids, they were loud
and long. Maxine and her sister dressed them
in baby clothes, named them after their mother's favorite
soap opera characters. They would eat anything.
Each day the girls would bring something new
to try—buttermilk soap, pencils, shoestrings,
hunks of liver, foil candy wrappers, fingernail clippings.
The goats entertained in their simple goat way.
They would not fetch a tennis ball, or curl up
on the screened porch bed for a nap with Maxine. One day
the goats were in the house, chewing the paper snowflakes
hung from fishing line across the hearth, a scattering of red
and green Monopoly houses, handfuls of dryer lint. They were wearing
Maxine's old dresses, now too small, even for her sister,
their floral patterns faded from hand-me-down existence.
At this moment, for the first time, Maxine could imagine herself
as a mother. That is until her own mother returned,
early from the market, finding goat shit
on the kitchen linoleum, and Erica Kane
swallowing a five dollar bill from a bowl by the front door.
Soon after, the goats were gone, sold to a neighbor,
Maxine realized that she liked only the idea of goats,
remembering them.

1976 Gonzales, California

This is not Italy, not these golden hills
tangled with the reaches of oak
that click with worms at the end of summer.
Two rows of eucalyptus trees line a dirt road.
The air is dry dust, tastes like the color brown.
Our fingernails are packed with farm dirt.
As we walk between perfectly spaced tree towers,
their pods fall like oxidized amusement park tokens,
thrown from a pier by a child, now washed
into barnacle beauties—rough and scented.

The pomegranate tree, shoulders sloped,
arms weighted, is dressed in heavy spots,
a rash of red. Every hanging circle is more
than an ornament, each is a swollen berry
ripe with its own secret fruits.
When halves are torn, two clusters of crimson
arils stain our chins and fingertips
a more delicate shade of blood,
the lipstick of childhood.

J.M. Barrie

It was over when he learned of mortal wounds,
a seven year old with a dead brother
whose perfect head had split on the ice,
like a peach thrown against a window.
His childhood, given over to dark
clothing, a heavy trench coat of guilt,
Wellingtons of grief. If there's one thing
losing prepares us for, it's more loss.
His ink and words, like homemade wrapping
paper, the sparkle and dressing
his own life lacked, tied tightly
enough to cut fingers tearing
knotted twine, forgetting the army knife
always in his trousers' pocket.
The lost boys, his adopted sons,
like his own brother—sudden spaces
on a page, every gap between things, from the hole
in the O, to that lonely hollow
curling just to the left of a question mark.
He was never young. Where did he go
to write? How could he hide?
A child behind a tree in a garden,
his eyes closed and covered,
waiting to be found.

Painless

A simple gift, from a godmother who misplaced her pouch of fairy dust. No golden glitter landed in sparkles on my head. She failed to wrap a leather Bible in tissue, or give me a wooden music box covered in sharp shells and blue seaglass. Here, she says, offering her empty palms, may you never feel pain.

I am discovered. A mass of beauty bruises, lengths of ribbon scars, imprint and incision, all scabs before they can heal. I raced my wooden wagon into trees, jumped from shed roof to trampoline, rode the zip line into the garage wall. It is not injury that I crave, but contact, the wounding moment. Adrenaline is my shocked audience, swallowing her cry, never screaming.

What I have become: defiant, senseless, willing to reach into a shrunken garden volcano erupting with fireants. I watch them trail bits of my skin to their queen, small attempts to steal my fingerprints. My blood, tiny velvet robes painted on divided bodies, dancing in a trail.

Look for the signs: display me under a fluorescent light, examine me. I am the forgotten masterpiece, roped off with velvet, alarmed. Hang me if you'd like. See my thick brushstrokes and layered pigment. No one wants to touch me until I'm crooked or fallen. Knock me down please.

The truth is: you cannot hurt me, nor do the stitches I pull out with my teeth, or the skin fused in band-aids, not even the sores that open and close like summer poppies. I am my own anaesthetic—always numb. The future is worry. What sparks will disfigure me? How deep can the blade be pushed in? Will I have a tendency towards shirtless men who will beat me? Will I tour the world with needles in my eyes? Will my answer always be yes?

A question that you should say yes to

Is the asking
more important than the question? What if
you forget to raise your voice
at the end of the sentence, like
a heavy kite tail, over-tied with ribbons,
no wind in the meadow?
If you had only asked me, if I
had only said, Is this a question?
Instead, the statement sat on the table
between us, a tiny, tarnished
trophy, both sets of our hands on its base.
What does the plaque say? Who wins
this award?
Just ask me.
And if I say yes, or nod, I will still
ask you to repeat the question. I like
the tones in your throat, the threads you
string the words on, and saying things
over makes them real.
Say it again.
Ask me.
I can't even think
of the letters that spell
no when I hear your voice.

Take it back,

this band of sapphires, set
in platinum, that I would wear
down to the thickness of thread,
or catch on my bureau's handle.
In thirty years it would slide off,
when I'm elbow deep
in potting soil, and I'd have to pour
our backyard through my sifter,
waiting for a clink or glint.
You'd have to replace me
with a woman who moves slowly, her big knuckles
armed with leather work gloves, and
the habit of touching thumb to fourth finger.
My dress, already vacuum-sealed in plastic,
is the casualty of plans, a shelved specimen
of my taste for imported lace, fabric
covered buttons, that my mother will keep
next to boxes of sailor suits, bunny pajamas,
a christening dress for her inconceivable
grandchild. Some will say I have bad
circulation, not enough blood to heat
my heart and feet, others will ask if I cried
while canceling the hall with high ceilings,
one hundred tables covered with wheat colored cloth,
six women in matching silk who already call me
by your last name, ivory paneled invitations
in bold antique Roman, and arrangements of tulips
tied with French ribbons, bows holding forever
in permanent wire knots. The date will pass
like Saturdays in August do, I will rise and open
windows to the morning smell of summer heat
about to be. I will trap the last cool air, slide shut
glass panes with latches, flip white shutters closed.

On my afternoon walk I will pop bubbles
in the street's soft tar, the sun hot enough
to fade bougainvillea, to burn
away the color of photographs,
from true to one tone of gray.

Bachelor Party

She is not unlike the child who awakens one morning with a keen interest in anatomy, asking, where does breakfast go when I swallow? How can I remember to blink? She never planned to be the cardboard wedding cake topping, she never aspired to pastry decorating. It just happened, the obscene jolt in her hips that got her thrown out of tap dancing lessons, an impulse to walk through the living room naked while her brother's friends stared at a football game, the bra straps she forced off her shoulders in the bathroom mirror. Not every girl yearns to be nude in a too lit hotel room where men lie on their backs biting dollar bills, waiting to have her knees remove their crumpled money. She says she's no hooker, her heart is not a lump of polished gold, she can't be bought. There is no dental hygienist night school, and no anemic child in need of braces. She invests saliva soaked cash in electrolysis, sequined pasties, leopard skin g-strings, velvet love seats, a puncture proof water bed mattress. She's fond of morning Vodka, her Corvette's blue leather interior, the body she's curved with needles and silicone. At stag parties she brings a gym bag containing one boom box, three erotic dance discs, ostrich feathers, a stack of washcloths, and seven cans of whipped cream. This is as intimate as it gets—after she undresses, the men lick cream off her shoulders, her stomach, her thighs. Her skin tastes tinny to them, a mixture of perfume and hair spray, all chemical. She thinks their tongues on her are no more than cats' mouths dipping into a milk bowl. She almost scalds herself in the shower afterwards. She pictures dozens of men walking into their dark bedrooms with the taste of her skin still on their lips; they go home to women who awaken and insist on being kissed goodnight.

Falling Senseless

for Carter Cooper

It's as if I'm wearing falconer's gloves, but I am leather—
thick, worn, yet pierceless. Once I was a living cow's hide
enduring a straw covered August hillside, without a single oak
to graze beneath. Now there are no senses in my fingertips,
not a tingle numb, not paralysis, it's just that when I touch
nothing registers: not the scorch of my morning shower,
not the bay wind—it only blows over my hair, pushes me.
Not my sheets pulled across my feet, tucked too tightly in the corners,
not the velvet cushions on mother's music room loveseat.
A kiss is torture, there is no pressure behind it, and I have nothing
to give back. My sense of taste slips as well, trips on my teeth,
scarring my tongue. I salt everything, but I am never thirsty.
I can no longer smell coffee, or bus exhaust. I open a bottle
of vanilla, a jug of ammonia, a tin of pipe tobacco. Nothing. Only
an odorless haze and a vague memory of my father's aftershave.
My hearing hasn't improved, although the sound of my own pulse
distorts other noises. Once I listened to each of mother's swallows,
could enjoy the piano two blocks away through open windows,
a student practicing Bach's requiem, and the chains from park swings
just across the street, their specific squeak and rattle, dragging
in the wind. Even when I am not asleep, my eyes won't fully open.
I no longer have peripheral vision. Every read sentence blurs,
and the portraits mother hung years ago are now just paint
patterns that run down the walls, as if they are trying to escape
their frames. For now, the only connection I have to anything
is gravity.

Reunion of the Separated

You belong to a boy who rode motorcycles. My chest tightens when engines rev, my pulse keeps time with the whirs and clicks of idle motors. I put my fingers on my throat to feel the bass of this song. I thought I knew who he was then, had dreams that a boy without a helmet performed fast gravel somersaults to be inside me. The medium told me the same, she smelled motor oil when she pricked my finger to look for features in my blood. He was wearing blue, she told me, jeans with a red tag on the back pocket, black tennis shoes, a striped navy and white sweatshirt. Before meeting her that morning I'd purchased a blue dress. I hated blue before surgery, never wore it—I was a pinched vein then, an oxygen starved baby, short one aorta. I had to squat to push blood through my legs, up to my brain.

I found his family while researching an obituary that matched my transplant date, the day my heart shriveled in the surgeon's hands like an overripe fruit, its bruised skin concealing rotten pulp. Until that moment the organ was a papier-mache piñata, and every pump of blood was a swing, freeing red wrapped candy from tearing layers. You came to me in an Igloo cooler, as inconspicuous as a six pack of beer—all eighteen years of brown feet on cement, a healthy diaphragm yell, a love for fried chicken. Now his mother tries not to stare at my chest when she speaks. She calls him by name occasionally, reminiscing over a bike contest he won, sharing news of his sister's engagement. I show her the scar. I would let her run her finger along its satiny seam if she asked. She cries and hugs me, a reminder that you are his heart, racing.

I've been sleeping with a younger man who has tattoos on his knuckles, firm legs, and a Harley-Davidson. When our bare chests meet I am closer to him than he knows. You, pomegranate-sized stranger, beat to another that could be your twin. I can't interpret your rhythm and flutter. Are you angry you weren't sewn into a man, delighted to be sitting behind handlebars again, or is this finally the marriage of our arteries, the steady rush of possession? My doctor puts the stethoscope to my ears, and I cry listening to our knocking, to you, my secondhand muscle. Oh to give you a voice. I am exhausted by these one-sided conversations. The cavity you fill never tried to speak before, there was only a hum where there's now your thudding murmur. Faithful partner, we touch only on the inside.

An inebriated monk illuminating a great text

The damp end of my sable brush, golden.
My teeth stained with cheap red table wine, consecrated
blood, or any deep liquid forgotten in a wooden chalice.
The entirety of my duty is replication, exacted
and measured in the increments of my drunkenness.
My gift from God: a steady hand. This brush, dipped
in jewel-toned paint, dragging down the manuscript
reminds me of a woman rising from the bath,
her hair in a point on her bare back.
These are not unholy figments, it is necessary
that I stay awake, find and interpret text
in candlelit silence. The only sounds: my swallowing,
scraping parchment, the occasional dropped palette.
I slur a prayer for better eyesight as I serve,
outlining His letters, following the Word.
My confession is that loneliness has wed despair,
in a poorly lit, unattended ceremony, and now
my penance is the proper comma, again and again,
the shape of a bleeding stigmata. My salvation—
knowing when to lift the brush handle
and sleep.

In a Goddamn Hotel Room

for Eugene O'Neill

The wallpaper peels like sunburnt skin,
errant patches of brown paint show through
where spots of red flocking were half glued.
A basin sits on your bureau, the pitcher a dull
blue, the color of your fingertips, stained
with ink from your fountain pen's gold nib.
The pine wardrobe wears the dents of someone
else's familiarity, its doors refuse to close,
like your sleeping mouth. White fringe
from the carpet's fraying edges lies
curled on the wooden floor, like scattered worms waiting
to crawl beneath your sheets, and sleep
in your eyes. Scentless, foreign cloth
encircles you. Your wife's ginger powder, the mint
colored cologne you slapped under your chin, soap
flakes smelling of eucalyptus, that sometimes stuck
in the pockets of your pants—all are
absent. The nightstand's marble top has chipped
corners. You keep a glass there, half filled
with murky Scotch, smudged with your damp fingerprints.
You reach for it in your sleep, spill on a letter
you ended, "A love that knows, Eugene."

Your eyes open to cracked plaster, and you remember
where you were born, the hotel at Broadway and 43rd. Your mother
took you once, to the room where she stained a mattress
silent maids covered minutes later with whiter sheets.
Your mother laughed when you asked her if she paid extra
for registering as one and leaving as two. You think
of when you checked in a week ago, barely able to sign your name,
leaning against the mahogany counter. You know you will
check out today on a stretcher, as nothing. It will not be
the first time you were carried through a hotel's front doors.

How do you choose your dying words? Are they a line you saved,
too perfect for stage direction? As you enunciate each
syllable are you actor or writer? Your face tightens
with rehearsed pain, your voice rises
with the final anger of leading men. You close
your life like you once closed theater curtains,
with one swift gesture, in this last place
that is not your own.

The right way to say goodbye

She leaves the motor running
not intending to end her own life,
but if she has to die to kill him,
so be it.

She leaves the motor running
not to warm the engine or fight frost,
not to hear its starting clicks, like fast spikes
in a footrace, the sound of a loud sprint
on pavement.

She leaves the motor running,
swings open the side door, and she is ajar.
Her ankles give way. She stretches out
on concrete, posed like a 40's movie siren
on a lake rock, delicate and still
in her modest bathing suit.

She leaves the motor running
breathing exhausted, useless air.
In the fumes she sees the shapes
of every letter that spelled his hard words,
each one outlined and weighted—the color
of smoke from burning tires.

She leaves the motor running,
while he sleeps across the vinyl bench seat,
the place he crawled from the bar curb.
He tried to hit her while she drove,
and his drunk aim left her hunched, flinching.

She leaves the motor running,
staying for the finality of it.
She waits a moment too long, a second
the length of a kiss.
How many times had they slept
in the same room after a fight?
She, in a heap on the floor
like an overcoat that missed the hook.
He, unwound, heavy limbs outstretched
in solid sleep—the kind that comes
fast and dark to those who don't know
how to forgive or regret.

Sound

I hear worms turning as they bury themselves in soil. I awaken to the sound of a plum's skin shedding. The inhaling and exhaling of birds distract me, their blue lungs boom as they fill with sky. I hear your muscles contract, snap like elastic, cramp into fists the size of baking apples. The veins in your wrists call to my heart, a syncopated code that says, "I'm in charge, you follow me."

In the morning there is nothing left of you but an imprint on the featherbed. Your outline reminds me of traced hands, Thanksgiving art projects in grammar school, fingers as feathers, thumb as head. Your giant thumbprint is set in the pillow beside me, the place your legs thrashed outside the comforter is plumage. I want to fill the space you left with plaster, to twist pipe cleaners around tissue flowers and commemorate your resting place. I want to hear memory fix itself with each popped bubble, as it dries. I want to capture each stirring of you.

What I do hear is a cat's spiney tongue catching hair and ticks, filtering out fluff and grime, the sound of cleansing and bristles. I hear my fingernails grow as they tap against glass, a steady creak against the cuticles, a tearing. I hear the moonlight through your skin, a glinty rhapsody of xylophones and tapped champagne glasses, all light notes, never a sharp or flat.

Obituary for a New York Corpse

the anonymous thunk of you
aloof on the median
against the Canadian barrier
the braille bumps dividing lanes
every vehicle accidentally
dissecting you
soul already ascended
disheartened by the very
flesh and bone of it all
the shred and burst
the tear and flattening
unrecognizable, inhuman
commuters convince themselves
you are part of a stray dog
you are only a shirt and a steak
fallen from a black garbage bag
blood is really brown paint
and you are only shadows
tricking sunrise eyes
only you know what happened
mistake or purpose
thrown or stumbled
pushed or tripped
high or suicidal
now the whole of you
simply pieces that can never fit together
a mess of DNA
a small paragraph
on the back page
of the New York Times

Iven Lourie

Growing Older Here

Photo by Nancy Christie.

Iven Lourie worked as Poetry Editor and Editor in Chief at *Chicago Review* literary journal in the 1960s, and he has pursued editing, writing, and performance art since that time. After completing his MFA at the University of Arizona (1978), where he studied with poets Richard Shelton and Peter Wild, he moved to Northern California where he still works as Senior Editor for Gateways Books, teaches composition at Sierra College, and leads creative writing classes. He has been married twice and has two daughters and one step-daughter. (Iven and Dick Lourie are the only 2-poet brother act in the *Directory of American Poets & Writers*.)

The Days of Awe

I. Rosh Hashannah

This is the day the world was created. I am so overjoyed to be here on this day. The world was created with a rose of an indescribable color, a sunrise rose, with the unmistakable fragrance of the First Rose. The world was created with a blue singing sky, with a few cottony slow motion clouds. A park with smooth green lawns, stone picnic benches, an empty baseball field with bleachers behind home plate. The world was created with families intact and broken. One father blows the ram's horn while his daughter next to him reads the formulaic words of the New Year ceremony.

The world was created on a day of remembrance, so it came complete with memories of other worlds. In these other worlds trout jump in a black river, jets take off and land at Orly Airport near Paris, farmers in straw hats bend over flooded rice paddies, a golden child plays with bottle caps in a dusty street in Capetown, masons chisel gargoyles for the roof of a cathedral, swimmers stare at the rainbow in a mountain waterfall, space ships land on Venus.

The world was created with pine boughs and bicycles, with robots and nail polish, with dolphins and teapots, with anger and pain, with ecstasies and embarrassments, with mushrooms and icebergs and electric guitars. The world was created with this notebook and a black pen and a little breathing time after a bowl of barley soup for lunch. The world was created today—and sure enough, I've been invited to a birthday party this evening.

II. The Raven

In September's hot Indian summer before *Yom Kippur* the raven arrived
We heard a commotion on the upstairs porch and a low churring sound
and there it was, sitting on the railing
It terrorized the cats, took over their territory, toyed with everything
not nailed down: paintbrushes, tools, bits of metal or leather, anything
shiny
It ate dry cat food, then once the children gave it kitchen scraps and
tidbits
the raven came back daily demanding more

Our friend Heather the storyteller said it was her friend Chief
Joseph
who appears as a raven, come to protect us from harm
We should honor him and give him tobacco and meat
Perhaps there is a specific harm he's come to ward off
or a specific message he has to communicate
One day he argued loudly in a tree with a turkey buzzard
who abandoned the territory to the raven

The grey fox on our dirt road has also been showing his graceful tail
more than we would have expected
Snakes and lizards abound in the last of summer sunshine
Even the deer grazing seem less timid, the young buck
standing beside the road is alert but wistful to say something
Could it be the next earthquake, a fire, an impending war, great changes
to come? Or something simpler, the thunderstorms of autumn?

We decided to feed the raven on the rocks beyond reach of dogs
It's visiting less, taking care of other neighborhood business perhaps
The danger may have been averted
or we may have absorbed the attack unknowingly
busy with our chores and watching the orange sky at sunset
Our wild companions may have something more to tell us
We wait for the return of Raven, their spokesperson

III. Monday, September 12, 1994

The planks shaking and rattling woke us up.
"Something big happened," Nancy said.
"No, it was someone tromping around on the upstairs porch."
5:27 A.M.
All the dogs in the area were barking
and the valley filled with the sound of cows moaning.
It was a Richter scale five-point-nine earthquake
near Lake Tahoe, less than one hundred miles away.

Last time I felt a tremblor on a visit with friends
years ago in Berkeley
it woke me up the same way.
I thought it was a heating furnace going on in the basement
that vibrated the house—
I went back to sleep

Which demonstrates that I might not know at all
what's going on in the case of an apocalypse.
Four horsemen spurring their mounts
and the heavens breaking open
might seem like a thunderstorm to me.
Or I could awaken from my own sudden death
and imagine I had nodded off over a novel
or that the odd landscape was produced by
summer heat and my eyeglasses that need to be replaced.

IV. Inventing the Pleasures

My partial inventory of the small pleasures of life:

Meeting someone by coincidence
Listening to the wind in the trees
Tasting a ripe, fresh fruit
Watching an entire sunset
Touching the hair of someone you love
Receiving or giving an unexpected gift
Talking to one's own child
Comforting an infant at night
Waking up in the morning outdoors

My friend Bruce Kaplan who died not long ago
told a story of a time in his life when
upon waking he'd put a foot down, carefully,
to see if the floor was there
As a clincher for this story (when he told it)
he claimed great affinity with a question posed
he said by the philosopher Wittgenstein:

"Why is there anything anyway?"

V. Honor Among Ghosts

In the days of awe at autumn and new moon of the Judaic calendar
our ancestors clamor louder for their due
The boundary between our world and theirs is thin
I see them driving those funny flat-fronted cars with big wheels
I see my great-grandparents lighting oil lamps and candles in the parlor
I see my grandfather fishing for eel in the Hudson River
and my grandmother cooking them in a huge pot
I see her feeding snails in a birdcage hanging in the kitchen

I see my great aunt's antique stall at the flea market in Paris
and the flowers at Blanc Mesnil where the socialist workmen
together bought their commune of gardens in the country
I see the Russian woman my father's mother sitting in a ladies' literary circle
reading Marx and Lenin until she had to leave the country
and I see the Russian man my father's father
burrowing deeper in the hay as a border guard
punches a pitchfork into the wagon checking for refugees

I see also the soot of bombs dropping on London and Dresden
and the nameless elders of my family with canes and bags
pushed against children in the train car leaving Paris for the East
the nameless aunts and uncles and cousins my Grandparents
never heard from again
I see the soot of coal stoves and soldiers' boots and the soot
from the concentration camp ovens blowing over Poland and Czechoslovakia

I hear the unassuming cry of my grandmother's little boy, a "crib death"
my infant uncle, and I hear his sister my mother again
singing "Suliram...ram...ram..." the lullaby just as The Weavers recorded
   it....
But the press and the clamor grow geometrically
Individual voices are indistinguishable in the keening and groaning
of the recent dead, their bodies piled up on TV and in magazines
the soot of mass cremations drifting, the new generation of trench graves

The voices aren't speaking Yiddish—they're Rwandan, Indonesian, Israeli,
Armenian, Bosnian, Romanian, Kurdish, Chinese, Sudanese, Lebanese
these ancestors newly dead
And many many many of the dead have no descendants to mourn them
no children surviving,
and many are children who never
had a chance to grow up
They press anxiously against the veil
their voices their longing and regrets so deep
they clamor and clamor for a way back into the playground of the living

This connection fades and goes quiet the walls harden
A rush of breath and of red blood pumps past millions of eardrums
The prayers recede and with them the ancestors' plaintive arms and hands
slip down the antechamber beaches into an indifferent ocean

The trouble is not that we can forget
or that their honor is diminished
It is that there are so many of the dead
already walking among us

VI. Fire Reflected in Water—*Yom Kippur* (Day of Atonement)

The Sentinels listen constantly—either confused or amused by humans'
misunderstanding of the hardness/softness dichotomy, the earth/fire
the water/air sometimes called the material-versus-immaterial question

Even the most idealistic people see the illusion of air as empty
the illusion of rocks trees and bodies in general as solid even if only
solid-seeming: the phantoms of their dreams or their solipsistic imaginations

The Sentinels stand so solid they are more invisible than the atmosphere
while our bodies shimmer and pour from one frame into another sometimes
leaving tracks of mercury or carnelian droplets in the iron-hard air

The cypress trees smoke and flicker on the hillsides the grass sparks
even boulders undulate with their remembered fires of carbon/silicon mobility
Across this holocaust of life burning bluer and whiter than younger created things

move the beings in their luminescence their fiery signatures threatening constantly
to disappear into the encroaching medium a closed hole or to drift up to hardened
space to journey toward fixed stars or to vaporize prematurely into random dust

The Sentinels wait and watch for the unlikely the unexpected yet inevitable event
They watch for the liquid oxygen being that flares and leaps up burning higher and
more intensely until its small flame merges with the One clear unfettered light

They motionless applaud and return to their implacable witnessing

A Question of Memory

> *I had my first dream in many months,*
> *confused but to this day imperishable,*
> *with a flute in it somewhere, and a*
> *wild goose, and a dancing girl.*
> —William Styron, *Darkness Visible: A Memoir of Madness*

When we're restored to health
as middle-aged or almost-senior men
the dreaming mind brings back
those best emblems of youth:

that nymph who takes off her clothes

one shooting star on a summer night
I tell my partner is Iris carrying a letter

the owl on a clothesline pole my grandmother
points to in the Pennsylvania morning mist
its hoot
             the pungent herbs and saltwater skin
mixed with smell of old blankets in a rented room
where when I reach to touch my wife
she dissolves into a nereid or a mermaid—
something feminine but hybrid

Would it be surprising then if after death
we rose up in another morning
shaking off the same seductive vestiges?

For Styron an exotic Salomé a haunting flute
the cry of a wild goose migrating south

For me that lithe greenish girl
who babysat us in summers, her eyes
sparkling as she leans over the Ausable River
the rush of water the pine resin the blue sky

The Daughter of Aeolus

Mykonos, Greece, 1998

The wind would be silent and quickly gone
except for the bamboo canes
The wind would smell only of the sea
except for the roses mimosa and mint
The wind would taste of salt and rainwater
except for the figs on the tree
the pomegranate the olives
the grapes of the vineyard

All these I would see and hear
smell taste and breathe
but forget each clean morning
except for my dream of the dark girl
wrapped in a towel
who sits on the bed and
brings her lips close to brush my cheek

This dream tells me the wind
the feta cheese tomatoes and wine
the dust of islands *thalassa* the sea
all are circulating in me
doing their work of inspiration and seduction

Comprehension

Rachel, your pale back and the dark
fall of hair are my wordless thoughts
You want me to speak from behind my eyes
more than my lips can know
Listen again
            A new language is made
from street talk and the speech of books
a lovely mobile struck from empty signs
Our breathing stirs it to delicacy
All the parts of us entwined in mottled light
are a tacit balance unseen in the world

Lee Bontecou Show at the Museum of Contemporary Art, Chicago

Upon entering I see that I know her work
have seen it in museums and magazines for decades
since I was a teenager
In retrospective I see that it is
an allegory of the soul
the same as all great art I have admired

She asserts fierce imagination's unconditional liberty
the eternality of mundane materials—canvas, iron,
copper wire, fabric, soot, clay, plastic....
Man Ray never judged a fellow artist
He would applaud her sincerity, her obsession,
her iconoclasm of means

I find in her work *The Human Universe* (from Charles Olson)
these hieroglyphics that both represent and embody
a cosmos ab novo / independently arising
an "imitation of nature"—but DID Aristotle mean playing God?
and "purposiveness without purpose" the translation
(to the best of my memory) of Kant's definition of art

I feel the haunting afoot in these galleries
the nightmare subtext the *vagina dentata*
I remember in 1958, in 1962, waking up from that dream—
factory corridors with monumental equipment running
a grey functional world inexorably encroaching on my light....

Her animals are dissected or exploded
There is change, mutation there is Hieronymous Bosch here
and Picasso's *Guernica* there is agony and joy
fused in bio-mimetic ecologies, revolving microcosms

I emerge from the subdued-light exhibit rooms
into a glass-windowed atrium
I see a bearded man
a woman in knee-high black vinyl boots
a Sikh couple with their little boy
who wears a cobalt blue turban

For the second time this month
I leave an art show in tears, tears
What is so sad or sentimental?
Is it the beauty itself?
Or the articulation of pain?
The transience?
Is all that one and the same?
Is it the life force of the artist in her artifact?

Now, I think like my wife, is the time
for a haiku summary:

Fish and spiky birds
Blown open by artist's joy—
City filled with rain

Winter Solstice

> *And even if you were in some prison the walls of which let*
> *none of the sounds of the world come to your senses—*
> *would you not then still have your childhood, that precious,*
> *kingly possession, that treasure-house of memories?*
> —Rainer Maria Rilke, Letters to a Young Poet

for Betty Lourie (1923-1975)

Nothing is as lofty and isolated as I remember it
especially Beth Sholom "The House of Peace" in Elkins Park
the Frank Lloyd Wright synagogue, towering concrete and glass

I stop first at the corner Chevron station
discover my elementary school on Montgomery Avenue
still an oblong brick building but diminutive

Nothing is left of immense walls and corridors I walked
"But the neighborhood hasn't changed much"
the Principal tells me   It's true

The family house is much the same: three stories
dormer windows of my bedroom under the roof
plaster lions where benches stood on our front porch

A blacktopped parking space is cut from our front yard
The ginkgo tree on the other side grown huge is empty
Its fan leaves scatter across the neighbor's lawn

In the backyard my mother's garden is gone—
no daffodils or roses, lilies or great hydrangea bushes
Only white porches and the basement trapdoor are familiar

but the entire scale of my childhood is gone and
the light   Leaning on the chain-link fence I cry
Mother has died, my mother is lost though here is

the clothesline an owl once sat on   I cry for my childhood
its excitement its warmth its colors and mysteries
those baby rabbits in a vast field beside the train tracks

now a patch of weeds and rubble
We died bullet-drilled to roll all the way down from
the suburban station's waiting room now just a few steps up

Instinctively I search my pocket for a penny to offer
on the rails for a train to flatten into an antique talisman
My eyes chill and harden after these tears

I find that I need my child-self to persist beyond this place
these sites in memory that are not real at all
My Elkins Park no longer exists

Still—my mother young and happy lives in my heart with
the rabbits the owl on the clothesline my daily companions
alongside irrelevant details: the fire trucks painted ivory white

Oh God help me—this fire burns in the memory
It forms a deathless crystal in the mind
Daughters and sons, brothers and sisters, listen:

I beg you to play and play and play as hard as you can
Be always curious no matter what they teach in school
Go find that wilderness outside next door it's so close

and it's yours to people with new better creations
This beauty this mystery of yours will last forever
It is your Self and it stays constant though the world burn

though the world shrink though it be drained of life
though it grow dull in mid-winter
bereft of parents and flowers

The Letting Go

9/11/2004—In Memoriam

I recently noticed that
a back spasm which kept me in acute pain
for several days and sent me to
the chiropractor for spine adjustment
had an unexpected after-effect:

when the pain receded even gradually
I experienced a surge of energy
a bubbling up of contentment
and exuberance—free again!

Then I found myself on a staircase
or stepping from a car door
imagining the emotion of a butterfly
breaking from the cocoon
a frog jumping on shore no longer fish-tailed
a locust or any crawling insect awakening
from its pupa dream to ride the air...

There may not be
another exhilaration to match
transforming the mode of being—
not just a snake leaving one skin
but a complete rejection

Dying then could be a leap
from this weighty realm into
some new element—
water—air—light—

and I hope for those who died
in that sudden fire
or who could only leap from windows
into the acrid air

that they had time to feel beyond resignation—
acceptance
and that they received their release from pain
as a liberation and a blessing

Growing Older Here

Once I wrote a letter to my Greek friend about living
in a crooked house in Saranac Lake New York
I wrote that while every place in Greece
has layers and layers of history buried under the present landscape
in rural NY State Vermont or Pennsylvania
we look out on a pristine landscape and humanize it each time
impose our own history on it like Charles Olson with his Yucatan

That was my ethos of a nomad—just keep trekking
break new ground find a new tribe next outpost
"move down move down clean cups clean cups"
Here I am in a new millennium 2001 Odyssey of a Poet
and somewhere along this lifeline the strategy changed

Fifteen years of my life or more in the Sierra Foothills
I'm aging here slowly perhaps but it catches up with you
Here the years of my life stack up in cords of firewood
scrub oak with some red manzanita mixed in
sunsets brilliant and garish over the Sutter Buttes
Units of time transform into stories—
The Year of the Valentine's Day Storm
with rifle shot branches falling
the power out for a week we melt snow for drinking water

The summer Wayne swept the big rattlesnake into a cardboard box
and drove it across the Yuba River up toward Sweet Land to let it go
The Summer of the 49er Fire when I helped pack an entire museum into
U-Haul trucks ready to run like hell before the fire line

Here the population explosion includes too many wild turkeys
deer that drift in herds around your lawn and garden
sounds of gunfire down in the ranchland bottom
lights in the sky
that could be UFO's or training flights out of Beale Air Force Base

All this is beautiful aesthetic dramatic sometimes satori in a quiet
improvisational key but I have to ask:
Where are the fires and snows of my prototype years?
What happened to the all night adrenalin talks
the birds flying missions of revelation in the dawn air?
the face of a lover refracting an entire spectrum of creation?
the sharp pain of not raising those two beautiful daughters of mine?
What happened to the Druid goddess of mysteries who made
that first holy pilgrimage with me from Pennsylvania to California?
What happened to the cosmic kaleidoscope of river water
rushing over ancient stones?
the breath of volcanoes crackling through my skin?
the spaceship of dreams zooming low through the coastal range?
What happened to "calling a spade a spade"?

Still the land wakes up new if I wait for it...

In these hills I have outlived my mother I should only grow to be as wise
I'm older than trench war casualty Guillaume Appolinaire God bless him
survived past Rimbaud's gun-running cut-short-by-gangrene middle age
I've outstripped (just in years...) Sylvia Plath Hart Crane
magnificent Gabriel Garcia Lorca
Look out you silverbeards I might face down your lifespans next:
old Walt Whitman who called grass "the hair of graves"
Allen Ginsberg gentle Dr. Williams writing as an old man
the most beautiful love poem I ever read
Marianne Moore "real toads in imaginary gardens..."

I am toeing the mark I'm eating more soy products
I'm studying Orion's belt from the hot-tub
I'm looking out over my backyard leach field pattern of weeds and star thistle
into the Pacific fogs
I am not as sharp as I was but aging in this place
has its own virtues and rewards
its dashing cowboy portico these roots that keep seizing air
these solar ruminations and architectonic stomach rumblings

Beyond Pilot Peak and the hawks bobbing on updrafts
I see the steppes of my Russian ancestors hallowed be your names too
I honor plant and animal fellow beings
I embrace geological eras planetary births galaxy explosions
I also become here less interesting to some old friends
simply part of the landscape
settled staying in place at rest
borrowing time
being marginal
getting old and garrulous
growing reflective in the Sierra Foothills

David McKay has been photographing in the Sierra for 38 years, and his work has been widely shown and published. He sees his photographs as a way to express the magic that happens when nature shares her secrets.

www.davidmckayphotography.com

www.ingramcontent.com/pod-product-compliance
Lightning Source LLC
Chambersburg PA
CBHW051803040426
42446CB00007B/499